The Emotiona

A Fail-proof Approach for Parenting, Understanding and Nursing a Traumatized Child

Larry Jane Clew

ISBN: 978-1-63750-231-0

Table of Contents

THE EMOTIONAL CHILD 1

INTRODUCTION 5

CHAPTER 1..7

    PARENTING AN EMOTIONALLY STRESSED CHILD..7

CHAPTER 2..11

    SIGNS OF EMOTIONAL STRESS IN CHILDREN 11

CHAPTER 3..15

    THE CONSEQUENCES OF CHILD YEARS TRAUMA..15

    Influence on Relationships...22

CHAPTER 4..25

    HOW TRAUMA AFFECTS CHILD DEVELOPMENT & BEHAVIOR: WHAT EDUCATORS NEED TO

    KNOW 25

    FIND YOUR PROGRAM...26

    HOW CHILDHOOD INJURY IMPACTS THE BRAIN...28

CHAPTER 5..33

    HELPING KIDS OF VARIOUS AGE GROUP TO RECOVER FROM EMOTIONAL STRESS............33

    HOW TO HELP CHILDREN AGE GROUPS 0-2..36

    HOW TO HELP CHILDREN AGE GROUP 2-5 37

    HOW TO HELP KIDS AGE GROUPS 2-5 DEAL WITH THE LOSS OF LIFE OF SOMEONE YOU CARE

    ABOUT: 42

    HOW TO HELP CHILDREN AGE GROUPS 6-11 42

    TYPICAL REACTIONS OF CHILDREN AGES 6 TO 11:....................................43

    HOW TO HELP KIDS OF AGE GROUPS 6-11 DEAL WITH THE LOSS OF LIFE OF SOMEONE: 48

    HOW TO HELP CHILDREN AGE RANGE 12-18 49

    TYPICAL REACTIONS OF CHILDREN AGES 12-18:......................................50

    HOW TO HELP KIDS AGE RANGE 12-18 DEAL WITH THE LOSS OF LIFE OF SOMEONE: 53

WHAT EDUCATORS CAN DO TO HELP STUDENTS 54

SIGNS OF INJURY IN CHILDREN & ADOLESCENTS 56

CHAPTER 6 ....**58**

HOW TO TREAT TRAUMATIZED CHILDREN 58

CHAPTER 7 ....**67**

4 METHODS TO START RECOVERY FROM CHILD YEARS TRAUMA 67

CHAPTER 8 ....**73**

LOOKING AFTER TRAUMATIZED CHILDREN 73

CHAPTER 9 ....**77**

HOW TO HELP A TRAUMATIZED CHILD IN THE CLASSROOM 77

Introduction

Do you know that children who experience emotional stress need to feel safe and loved?

All parents desire to provide this type of thriving home for their children and family. However, when parents don't have the right understanding of the consequences of trauma, they could misinterpret their child's behavior and find themselves frustrated or resentful.

Their efforts to address troubling behavior in their children may be ineffective or, in some instances, even harmful and subsequently make parenting horrible.

This is why this book is aimed at helping parents understand the trauma their children may be going through and build the right mindset and attitude to address and relate with their children with care, and love.

This book is about how to nurture and understand the signs of trauma and stress in children, tips for helping kids of various age group, consequences of child years trauma, how to treat traumatized children, and many more!

By upping your understanding of their emotional stress and trauma, you can help support your child's recovery without any hassle.

After reading this book, you would have learned how to burse your emotional child and raise a thriving child under no stress on your part as a father or mother.

This book is likewise recommended for intending father or mother.

Chapter 1

Parenting an Emotionally Stressed Child

Children who have experienced emotional stress need to feel safe and loved. All parents want to provide this type of nurturing home for their children. However, when parents don't have an understanding of the consequences of trauma, they could misinterpret their child's behavior and find themselves frustrated or resentful.

Their efforts to address troubling behavior may be ineffective or, in some instances, even harmful. This factsheet talks about the type of trauma, its results on children and youngsters, and ways to help your son or daughter.

By upping your understanding of stress, you can help support your child's recovery, your relationship with her or him, as well as all your family together.

What is Trauma?

Trauma can be an emotional response to an extreme event that threatens or causes damage. The damage can be physical or psychological, real or recognized, and it can threaten the kid or someone near her or him.

Trauma could possibly be the result of an individual event, or it can derive from contact with multiple events as time passes.

Potentially traumatic events can include:

- Abuse (physical, intimate, or psychological)
- Neglect
- Ramifications of poverty (such as homelessness or devoid of enough to consume)
- Being separated from family members
- Bullying
- Witnessing injury to someone you care about or family pet (e.g., domestic or community assault)
- Natural disasters or accidents
- Unstable parental behavior credited to dependency or mental illness.

For most children, being in the kid welfare system becomes another traumatic event. That is true of the child's first separation from his/her home and family, as well as any extra placements.

The Impact of Untreated Trauma

Children are resilient. Some stress in their lives (e.g; departing caregivers for a trip to school, buttoning a shirt for the first time, feeling anxious before a casino game or performance) helps their brains to develop and new skills to build up.

However, by definition, trauma occurs whenever a stressful experience (such as being abused, neglected, or bullied) overwhelms the child's natural capability to deal. These events result in a "fight, airline flight, or freeze" response, resulting in changes in the body-such as faster heart rate and higher bloodstream pressure as well as changes in the way the brain perceives and responds to the world.

Frequently, a child's body and brain recover quickly

from a potentially traumatic experience without lasting

damage. However, for other children, injury interferes with normal development and can have long-lasting effects.

Chapter 2

Signs of Emotional Stress in Children

In the week of the disturbing event or tragic loss in the lives of children, we realize parents and teachers can do their finest to help kids cope using their grief and anxiety in a wholesome way. We've provided some tips about how best to participate kids in a relaxed and supportive dialog about their feelings; it's definitely not easy to do, but it can make a tremendous difference to kids.

Still, some children are more in danger than others for suffering long-term effects from an upsetting event, including those people who have lost good friends or classmates and the ones who may have learned about the function or loss in an emotional and upsetting way.

"What sort of child experiences a meeting and exactly how those around him handle it have an impact on how traumatizing it could be", records, Child Brain Institute psychologist Dr. Jerry Bubrick. When households come upon information unintentionally, parents can be captured off safeguard and react in an extremely psychological way that can impact children. Television coverage and surprising newspaper headlines can also amplify the impact of the troubling event or reduction.

So even while you make an effort to soothe and comfort children, it's important to identify the signs of harmful coping that could suggest a visit with a specialist might be needed. In acute cases, children can form post-traumatic stress disorder, but even less extreme PTSD-like symptoms can hinder a child's life and joy. Below are a few signs to consider and what to keep in mind.

- **Normal Grief**

"Everyone grieves at a different speed," Dr. Bubrick says, and an instantaneous reaction or insufficient one is not necessarily an indication of what sort of child will deal with losing. "If a kid appears to be coping well now, they could still have an unhealthy response later," he says.

Everyone grieves at a different speed

"Or it might also be you who needs to be an indicator

that they're handling it well." So while you want to help our kids whenever you can immediately after the function, an enduring and hurtful response usually won't be obvious until three or six months later.

- *Increased considering death and safety*

One common indication of PTSD or a PTSD-like response is exactly what Dr. Bubrick phone calls a "hyper-focus on mortality or loss of life." Even though some kids become notably morbid and fascinated with death, others will establish an obsession using their security and the protection of those near to them. Regarding an open fire or another catastrophe, their thoughts might come back with troubling regularity to the probability of a fireplace in their own house, or of the earthquake or overflow happening their current address.

- *Issues with sleeping, eating, anger, and attention*

A number of the symptoms of injury in children (and adults) closely mimic depressive disorder, including too much or inadequate sleep, lack of hunger or overeating, unexplained irritability and anger, and problems concentrating on projects, assignment work, and discussion. Sometimes the symptoms show up similar to a panic disorder, obsessive or pervasive concern with difficulty separating from parents.

- *Triggers*

Twelve months after a tragic event, we tend to look back again, take stock, and memorialize those whose lives were lost. But as Dr. Bubrick observes, there are other anniversaries linked to children's lives that could have unpredicted effects for them; the birthdays of friends or classmates who passed away, for example. "Children could be essentially OK between occasions, maybe with some rocky intervals," he says. "And around enough time of the birthday, they could have significantly more symptoms. It's a result."

Chapter 3

The Consequences of Child Years Trauma

Although adults often say things such as, *"He was so young when that happened. He won't even keep in it mind as a grown-up."* Childhood stress can have a long term effect. Even though kids are resilient, they're not manufactured from stone.

That's not saying your son or daughter will be psychologically scarred forever if he/she endures a horrific experience. With appropriate interventions, adults can help kids get over traumatic experiences better.

But it's important to identify whenever your child might need specialized help with working with stress. Early treatment could stop your child from experiencing ongoing ramifications of the trauma as a grown-up.

What is it?

Various encounters can constitute trauma. Physical or

intimate misuse, for example, can be obviously distressing for children.

Onetime events, just like a car crash or an especially severe natural disaster (such as a hurricane, for example), may take a mental toll on children as well.

Ongoing stress, such as residing in an unhealthy neighborhood or being the victim of bullying, can be traumatic, even if it just feels as though lifestyle to a grown-up. Almost any event can be viewed as traumatic to a kid if:

- It just happened unexpectedly.

- It just happened repeatedly.

- Someone was intentionally cruel.

- The kid was unprepared for this.

Childhood injury also doesn't have to occur directly to the kid; for instance, viewing someone you care about suffer can be hugely distressing as well. Contact with violent press can also traumatize children.

Just because an event is upsetting, however, doesn't make it traumatic. Parental divorce, for example, will probably affect a kid, but it isn't always traumatize.

It's also important to keep in mind that a child endured a tragedy or a near-death experience, doesn't mean he/she'll automatically be traumatized. Some kids are significantly less suffering from their circumstances than others.

When it leads to PTSD

Many children face distressing events at one point or another. While the majority of them experience problems following a distressing event, almost all of them go back to a normal condition of working in a comparatively short time.

However, many children, usually between three and fifteen percent of ladies, and one to six percent of boys develop post-traumatic stress disorder (PTSD).

Children with PTSD may re-experience the stress in their thoughts again and again. They could also avoid whatever reminds them of the injury, or they could re-enact their stress in their play.

Sometimes children believe they missed indicators predicting the traumatic event. In order to prevent future traumas, they become hyper-vigilant in looking for indicators that something terrible will happen again.

Children with PTSD could also end up having:

- Fear.

- Depression.

- Anxiety.

- Anger and aggression.

- Self-destructive behavior.

- Emotions of isolation.

- Poor self-esteem.

- Difficulty trusting others.

Even children who don't develop PTSD may still exhibit

psychological and behavioral issues carrying out a distressing experience. Below are a few things to look out for through the weeks after an upsetting event:

- Increased thoughts about death or safety.

- Problems sleeping.

- Changes in appetite.

- Anger issues.

- Attention problems.

- School refusal.

- Somatic complaints like headaches and stomachaches.

- Loss of desire for normal activities.

- Irritability.

- Sadness.

- Development of new fears.

- Influence on Long-Term Health.

- Traumatic events make a difference in what sort of child's brain develops, which can have long term consequences.

Studies also show that the greater adverse childhood encounters one has, the bigger their threat of health and fitness problems later in life. Years as a child injury may increase an individual's threat of:

- Asthma.

- Depression.

- Cardiovascular system disease.

- Stroke.

- Diabetes.

Additionally, a report published in 2016 in Psychiatric Times noted that the prevalence of suicide attempts was significantly higher in adults who experienced trauma, such as physical abuse, sexual abuse, and parental domestic violence, as a kid.

Influence on Relationships

A child's relationship, along with his caregiver, whether his parents, grandparents, or otherwise, is essential to his emotional and physical health. This romantic relationship and connection help the tiny one figure out how to trust others, manage feelings, and connect to the world around them.

Whenever a child encounters an injury that shows him/her that he/she cannot trust or rely on that caregiver, however, the child is more likely to think that the world around him is a scary place and every adult are dangerous, and that means it is incredibly difficult to create relationships throughout their child years, including with peers of their age, and into the adult years.

Children who battle to maintain healthy accessories to caregivers will probably struggle with intimate associations during adulthood. Australian research greater than 21,000 child mistreatment survivors, age group 60 and old, reported an increased rate of failed relationships.

How to help:

Family support can be vital to lowering the impact stress has on children. Below are a few ways to aid a kid after an upsetting event:

- Encourage your son or daughter to discuss his feelings and validate his emotions.

- Answer questions honestly.

- Reassure your son or daughter that you'll do all you can to keep him safe.

- Adhere to your day to day routine whenever you can.

If your son or daughter has been subjected to traumatic circumstances, and you've noticed changes in her feeling or behavior, speak to her pediatrician. Your physician can assess your child's health insurance and, if required, make a referral for mental health treatment.

Based on your child's age group and needs, he/she may be known for services such as cognitive behavioral therapy, play therapy, or family therapy. Medication can also be a choice to take care of your child's symptoms.

Chapter 4

How Trauma affects Child Development & Behavior: What Educators Need to know

Online Experts MS Programs in Early Child years Studies Source shows how stress affects child development and behavior, and what years as a child educators need to find out.

Graduates of early years as a child education level programs can find the skills and knowledge to identify the telltale indications of injury in children.

Speaking with a counselor, children can experience stress from many directions; Natural disasters devastate areas, leaving family members homeless. Children are captured in the crosshairs of shootings and community assaults. However, the most prominent psychological storms neglect and abuse rage inside the house, where children are likely to feel safe and adored. Despite the fact that adults experience injury too, maturity helps them process the occasions better and go back to a feeling of normalcy.

For children, early-life traumas can, in fact, alter their young brains and lead to developmental and behavioral problems.

Without a close relationship with parents and other caregivers, children learn they cannot rely on one to help them. If they are exploited and abused, children think that these are bad, and the world is unsafe and awful. Trauma impairs the standard development of the mind and anxious system, the disease fighting capability, and the body's stress response systems.

Walden Offers 80+ Online Programs to go Your Life Forwards, find your program now.

Find Your Program

- Indicators of Early Youth Trauma

Early childhood educators can play an important role in observing, identifying, and advocating for children who show signs of trauma in daycare, preschool, kindergarten, and primary school settings. It's important to understand common symptoms of trauma like the following:

Children up to 24 months old often:

- Demonstrate poor verbal skills.

- Exhibit memory space problems.

- Screen an excessive temper.

- Scream or cry excessively.

- Exhibit regressive actions.

Children 3-6 years of age often:

- Have trouble learning or concentrating in school.

- Develop learning disabilities.

- Demand attention through negative and positive behaviors.

- Are verbally abusive.

- Experience stomachaches and headaches.

Without early intervention and help, traumatized children grow up to be traumatized adults, often having abnormal reactions to stress, chronic physical ailments, relationship problems, learning difficulties, and tendencies to activate in risky behaviors like substance abuse and lawbreaking.

How Childhood Injury impacts the Brain

Distressing stress impacts the growing brains of men and women differently, in accordance with a new study from the Stanford University School of Medicine and the first Life Stress and Pediatric Anxiety Program.

In youth with symptoms of post-traumatic stress, there is certainly variation in the quantity and surface of the insula between men and women who have experienced distressing stress versus those people who have not, the analysis found. *The insula is an area buried deep within the cerebral cortex that takes on an integral role interoceptive digesting (how much or how little attention one will pay to sensory information in the body), feelings rules, and self-awareness.* The analysis was released online in the journal; Depressive Disorder and Stress on January 9. It's the first research to date, which includes examined sex distinctions in subdivisions of the insula in youngsters with stress histories.

Even though many individuals experience trauma, curiously, not absolutely all of these develop post-traumatic stress disorder (PTSD). Folks who are identified as having PTSD or experienced a distressing stressor in their lives withstand exposure to real or threatened loss of life and "intrusive" thoughts afterward, that are from the distressing event. These intrusive symptoms are coined such because they're unwanted and unwelcome by the average person who encounters them and include repeated, involuntary distressing remembrances, dreams, flashbacks, and extreme, prolonged mental and physiological reactions, as though the distressing event were still happening (though it has long ceased). Subsequently, the individual subjected to injury who is susceptible to developing PTSD will avoid any stimuli from the distressing event and can experience changes in thought and disposition, as well as regularly heightened arousal (APA, 2013). Earlier neuroscience research has discovered that changes in the insula pursuing stress contribute not and then the introduction of PTSD, but also to its maintenance. Likewise, it was discovered that women who experience injury would develop PTSD (Hanson et al., 2008), but researchers have never had the opportunity to pinpoint why... as yet.

Fifty-nine youth between the ages of nine and seventeen participated in the analysis. Half of the individuals exhibited PTSD symptoms, and half didn't. The two stress versus no-trauma organizations had similar age group, IQ, and sex characteristics. From the 30 individuals (14 women and 16 men) with injury, 5 reported one distressing stressor, as the remainder (n=25) reported more than two distressing stressors or chronic stress publicity. Using structural magnetic resonance imaging (SMRI), experts scanned the individuals' brains and likened healthy male and feminine brains to the brains of men and women with PTSD symptoms. Though there have been no structural variations in insula subdivisions between healthy male and female brains, there have been notable distinctions between men and women in the traumatized group. Males with injury had larger insula quantity and surface than males in the control group, while women with stress experienced smaller insula quantity and surface than young ladies in the control group. This finding shows that injury not only affects the developing brain but also that it influences the introduction of children quite differently.

Insula volume lowers with aging (Shaw et al., 2008), and the reduced insula quantities in ladies with PTSD symptoms shows that this area of the brain is prematurely aging in part credited to distressing stress. Klabunde, Weems, Raman, & Carrion (2017) drove home the need for these results in their paper:

"By better understanding sex variations in an area of the mind involved with emotion control, clinicians and scientists might be able to develop sex-specific stress and emotion dysregulation treatments."

The analysis also helps highlight the interplay between character and nurture as it pertains to assessing complex mental medical issues, such as PTSD. Some people do not easily get access to equipment such as an MRI scanning device used to elucidate this study's results, mental medical researchers and patients as well be capable of understanding that environmental stress means neurobiological changes and these changes differ between your sexes, meaning a one-size-fits-all method of PTSD will be significantly less effective when compared to a treatment which considers contextual factors of the average person, such as natural sex.

Chapter 5

Helping Kids of Various Age Group to Recover from Emotional Stress

Recognize that questions may persist: As the aftermath of a tragedy can include constantly changing situations, children may have questions more sometimes; tell them you will be ready to chat anytime. Children need to break down information independently, timetable and questions might emerge from nowhere.

Encourage family conversations about the loss of life of someone you care about: When family members can chat and feel unfortunate together, it's much more likely that kids will talk about their feelings.

Do not give children too much responsibility: It is vital never to overburden kids with jobs, or provide them with adult ones, as this is too stressful for them. Instead, for the longer term, you should lower anticipations for household responsibilities and school needs, though it is good to keep these things to do, at least some tasks.

Give special help to kids with special needs: These children may necessitate additional time, support, and assistance than other children. You may want to simplify the vocabulary you utilize and do it again frequently. You may even need to tailor information to your child's power; for instance, a kid with language impairment may better understand information by using visible materials or other methods of communication you are accustomed to.

Watch for indicators of trauma: Within the first month after a tragedy, it's quite common for kids to appear mostly okay. From then on, the numbness wears off, and kids might experience more symptoms, especially children who have witnessed accidental injuries or loss of life, lost of immediate family, experienced previous stress in their lives, or who aren't resettled in a fresh home.

Know when to get help: Although stress and other issues may last for weeks, seek immediate help from your loved ones' doctor or a mental doctor if indeed they do not abate, or your son or daughter starts to listen to voices, views things that aren't there, becomes paranoid, encounters anxiety attacks, or has thoughts of attempting to damage himself or other folks.

Look after yourself: You are able to help your son or daughter best when you do yourself a favour. Discuss concerns with friends and family members; it could be beneficial to form a support group. If you participate in a chapel or community group, keep taking part; make an effort to eat right, drink sufficient water, stick to exercise sessions, and get enough rest. Physical health protects against psychological vulnerability. To lessen stress, do yoga breathing. If you have problems with severe panic that inhibits your ability to operate, seek help from a health care provider or mental doctor, and if you don't get access to one, talk to a religious innovator. Recognize your dependence on help and obtain it. Get it done for your child's sake, if for no other reason.

How to Help Children Age groups 0-2

Infants sense your feelings and react accordingly: If you're calm, your child will feel secure. If you take action stressed and overwhelmed, your child may react with fussing, trouble being soothed, eat or rest irregularly or may be work withdrawn.

Your skill:

- Try your very best to act relaxed. Even though you are feeling pressured or anxious, speak to your baby in a calm voice.

- Respond regularly to your baby's needs. The developmental job of this age group is to trust caregivers so kids can form a solid, healthy attachment.

Continue nursing if you have been breastfeeding. Although there's a myth that whenever a mother encounters shock, her breast milk becomes bad and may cause the infant to be "sluggish" or have learning disorders, that's not true. It's important to continue medicals for your child to keep him or her healthy and linked with you. You will need to remain healthy to breastfeed, so do your very best to consume enough and drink clear water.

Consider your baby's eye, smile at him/her, touch him/her. Research demonstrates vision contact, touch, and being in a mother's existence helps maintain a baby's feelings balanced.

How to Help Children Age group 2-5

As of this age, although children are making significant developmental improvements, they still depend on parents to nurture them. Much like infants, they typically react to situations relating to how parents react. If you're calm and assured, your son or daughter will feel better. If you act stressed or overwhelmed, your son or daughter may feel unsafe.

Typical reactions of children ages 2 to 5:

- Speaking repeatedly about the function or pretending to "play" the function.

- Tantrums or irritable outbursts.

- Crying and tearfulness.

- Increased fearfulness, often of the dark, monsters, or being alone.

- Increased sensitivity to appearance like thunder, wind, and other noises.

- Disruptions in eating, sleeping, and toileting.

- Thinking that the catastrophe can be undone.

- Extreme clinging to caregivers and trouble separating.

- Reverting to early behavior like baby speak, bed-wetting, and thumb-sucking.

Your Skill:

Make your son or daughter feel safe: Keep, hug, and cuddle your son or daughter whenever you can. Inform her you will look after her when she feels unhappy or frightened. With children who understand how to speak, use simple phrases such as "Mommy's here."

Monitor what you say: Small children have big ears and may detect your anxiousness, misinterpret what they hear, or be frightened unnecessarily by things they don't understand.

Maintain routines whenever you can: No matter what your living situation is, do your very best to have regular mealtimes and bedtimes. If you're homeless or have relocated, create new routines. Make an effort to do the items you have always finished with your kids, such as performing songs or stating prayers before each goes to sleep.

Give extra support at bedtime: Children who have been through injury may become stressed during the night. When you put your son or daughter to bed, spend additional time than typical talking or informing stories. It's alright to produce a temporary set up for small children to rest with you, but with the knowledge that they will get back to normal, set sleeping plans at an arranged future date.

Do not expose kids to the news headlines: Young kids tend to confuse facts with worries. They might not recognize that the images they see on the news headlines aren't happening over and over. They also need not to pay attention to the radio.

Encourage children to talk about their feelings: Get one of these simple questions such as, "How are you feeling today?" Follow any discussions about the recent event with a favorite tale or a family group activity to help kids feel more secure and calm.

Enable your son or daughter to tell the story plot of what happened: this can help him/her seem sensible of the function and deal with their emotions. Play can frequently be used to help your son or daughter frame the story plot and inform you of the function in her own words.

Draw pictures: Small children often prosper, expressing feelings with drawings. That is another chance to provide explanations and reassurance. To start a discussion, you might comment on just what a child has attracted.

If your son or daughter acts out, it might be an indicator she needs extra attention: Help her name how she feels: Frightened? Angry? Sad? Let her know it is alright to believe that way, then show her the proper way to behave. You can say, "It's alright to be upset, but it isn't okay going to your sister."

Get kids involved with activities: Distraction is an excellent thing for kids as of this age group. Play video games with them, and request playtime with other kids.

Discuss things that are going well: Even in the most attempting times, it's important to recognize something positive and communicate hope for the near future to help your son or daughter recover. You are able to say something similar to, "We still have one another. I am here with you, and I'll stick with you." Pointing out the nice, can help you feel better too.

How to help kids age groups 2-5 deal with the loss of life of someone you care about:

Talk with them at their level: Use similar encounters to help children understand, like the death of the family pet or changes in plants in your garden.

Provide simple explanations: For instance, "When someone dies, we can't see them any longer, but we can still take a look at them in pictures, please remember them."

Reassure your kids: They could feel what occurred is their problem, somehow, tell them it isn't.

Expect repeated questions: That's how small children process information.

How to help Children Age groups 6-11

At this age, children are more in a position to discuss their thoughts and emotions and can better deal with difficulties; however, they still turn to parents for comfort and assistance. Hearing them demonstrates your dedication when frightening things happening could be the most reassuring thing for a frightened child.

Typical reactions of children ages 6 to 11:

- Anxiety.

- Increased aggression, anger, and irritability (like bullying or fighting with peers).

- Sleep and hunger disturbances.

- Blaming themselves for the function.

- Moodiness or crying.

- Concerns about being looked after.

- Concern with future damage or loss of life of family members.

- Denying the function even occurred

- Issues about physical pain, such as stomachaches, headaches, and lethargy, which might be thanks to stress

- Frequently asking questions

- Refusing to go over the function (more typical among kids age range 9 to 11)

- Withdrawal from sociable interactions

- Educational problems: Trouble with memory and concentration at school, refusing to wait in school.

Your skill to help:

Reassure your son or daughter that he/she is safe: Children of this age group are comforted by facts; use real words, such as hurricane, earthquake, overflow, aftershock. For kids of this age group, knowledge is empowering and helps relieve stress and anxiety.

Keep things as "normal" as you possibly can: Bedtime and mealtime routines help kids feel safe and sound. If you're homeless or have been relocated, set up different routines, and present your son or daughter some choice in the matter. For example, let your child choose which tale to inform at bedtimee; thus giving a child a feeling of control during an uncertain time.

Limit contact with TV, papers, and radio: The greater the bad information school-age kids face, the more concerned they'll be. Information, video footage can magnify the stress of the function; so whenever a child will watch an information report or pay attention to the radio, sit down with him/her, and that means you can discuss it afterward. Avoid allowing your son or daughter to see visual images.

Spend time speaking with your son or daughter: You're your child that it's alright to ask questions and also to exhibit concerns or sadness. One method to encourage conversation is by using the family time (such as mealtime) to discuss what is occurring in the family as well as locally. Also, ask what his friends have been stating, which means you can be sure to right any misinformation.

Answer questions briefly, but honestly: After a kid has taken something up, first require his ideas, and that means you can understand precisely what the concern is. Usually, children ask a question because they're concerned about something specific. Provide a reassuring answer. If you don't know a remedy to a question, it is alright to state, "I don't know." Usually, do not speculate or do it against rumors.

Acquire children who do not speak: Open a conversation by posting your feelings; for example, you could say, "This is a very frightening thing, and sometimes I awaken in the night time because I am in a great deal of thought. How are you feeling?". Doing this can help your son or daughter feel he/she is not by him/herself in his/her concerns. However, do not provide a lot of fine detail about your anxieties.

Keep children occupied: Day to day activities, such as using friends or heading to school, might have been disrupted. Help kids think of option activities and organize playgroups with other parents.

Relaxed worries about friends' safety: Reassure your kids that their friends' parents are caring for them just because they are being looked after by you.

Discuss community recovery: Let children know that things are being done to keep them safe, or restore electricity and drinking water and that authorities and community organizations are assisting, if applicable.

Encourage kids to assist: This gives them a feeling of achievement and purpose at the same time when they could feel helpless. Youngsters can do small duties for you; old ones can donate to volunteer tasks locally.

Find the wish: Children need to start to see the future to recuperate. Kids this age group appreciate specifics. For instance, in case of natural devastation, you could say: "Folks from coast to coast are sending medical materials, food, and drinking water. They've built new places where folks who are harm will be taken care of, and they'll build new homes. Things may be very difficult limited to only a little while."

How to help kids of age groups 6-11 deal with the loss of life of someone:

Uncover what your son or daughter is considering: Ask questions before you make assumptions about what your child desires to know. For instance, you can say, "It made me so upset when grandma passed away. How about you? It's hard to take into account, isn't it?"

Use real words: Avoid euphemisms for loss of life like "He visited a much better place." School-age children are often confused by hazy answers. Instead, you can say, "Grandma has passed away, she actually is not returning, which is alright to feel unfortunate about this."

Be as sincere as you can: Use simple drawings to spell it out, things like the body and accidents.

Inform your son or daughter: Let her know that anger and sadness are typical, which if she avoids emotions, she may feel even worse later on.

Ready your child for anticipated changes in routines or household functions. Discuss what the actual changes mean for him/her.

Reassure your son or daughter: Help him/her understand it is alright, and normal, to have a problem with college, peers, and family during this time.

Encourage meaningful memorializing: Pray collectively as a family group and take your son or daughter with you to the Chapel to light a candle. Your son or daughter may also want to create a notice to the deceased person or attract an image you can hang up the phone.

Show patience: Kids up to age group eleven may think the loss of life is reversible and can have trouble taking the actual fact that the individual may not come back. You may want to say frequently, "He died, and it is not returning, and I am unhappy."

How to help children age range 12-18

Adolescence has already been a challenging time for teenagers who have so many changes taking place in their bodies. They have a problem with seeking more self-reliance from parents, and also incline to feel nothing at all could harm them. Distressing events can make sure they feel uncontrollable, even if indeed they act as if they're strong. They'll also feel bad for individuals suffering from the disaster, and also have a solid desire to learn why the function occurred.

Typical reactions of children ages 12-18:

- Avoidance of feelings.

- Regular rumination about the disaster.

- Distancing themselves from relatives and buddies.

- Anger or resentment.

- Depression, as well as manifestation of suicidal thoughts.

- Freak out, including fretting about the future.

- Feeling swings and irritability.

- Changes in urge for food and,or rest habits.

- Academics issues, such as trouble with memory and concentration, and or refusing to wait in school.

- Involvement in risky or unlawful behavior, like alcohol consumption

Your skill:

Make your child feel safe again: Children do nothing like showing vulnerability; they could try to act as if they're doing fine even though they aren't. While they could withstand hugs, your touch can help them feel secure. You are able to say something similar to, "I understand you're produced now, but I simply need to offer a hug."

Help teenagers feel helpful: Provide them with small jobs and obligations in family members, then compliment them for what they did and exactly how they have dealt with themselves.

Do not overburden teenagers with way too many duties, especially adult-like ones, as that will increase their anxiety.

Open the entrance for discussion: It's very typical for teenagers to state they don't want to chat. Try to begin a conversation when you are doing a task together, so the conversation will not feel too extreme or confrontational.

Consider peer organizations: Some teens may feel convenient talking in groupings with their peers, so consider arranging one. Also, encourage discussion with other respected adults, just like a relative or instructor.

Limit contact with Television, papers, and radio: While teenagers can better deal with the news headlines than more youthful kids, those who find themselves struggling to detach themselves from television or the air may be attempting to cope with nervousness in harmful ways. Regardless, talk with your child about the items he/she has seen or noticed.

Help your child do something: Kids of this age group would want to help the city. Find appropriate volunteer opportunities.

Be familiar with substance abuse: Teenagers are particularly in danger for embracing alcoholic beverages or drugs to numb their stress. If your child has been behaving secretively or is apparently drunk or high, speak to a health care provider. And speak to your young in a sort way. For instance, People often drink or use drugs after a tragedy to quiet themselves or forget, but additionally, it may cause more problems. Various other actions you can take are to go for a walk, speak to friends and family about how you are feeling, or reveal your expectations for a much better future.

How to help kids age range 12-18 deal with the loss of life of someone:

Be patient: Teenagers may have a concern with expressing feelings about death. Cause them to talk by stating something similar like, "I understand it is terrible that grandma has passed away. Experts say it's good to talk about our emotions. How are you doing?"

Be very open: Discuss the ways you are feeling; the loss of life may be influencing his/her behavior.

Be flexible: It is okay, at the moment, to indeed have a

little more versatility with guidelines and educational and behavioral objectives.

Memorialize meaningfully: Pray jointly at home, let your child light a candle at the cathedral. You need to include him/her in memorial ceremonies; he/she may also appreciate performing a private family tribute at home.

What Educators can do to help Students

Resume routine whenever you can: Children tend to work better when they know very well what to expect. Time for a school regular can help students believe that the troubling occasions have never used control over every part of their daily lives. Maintain the targets of students. It doesn't have to be a hundred percent, but having to do some homework and simple classroom tasks are very useful.

Be familiar with signs, a child might need extra help: Students who cannot function credited to emotions of extreme sadness, dread, or anger should be described to a mental doctor. Children may have stress that is manifested as physical illnesses, such as mind pains, stomach aches, or extreme exhaustion.

Help kids understand more about what happened: For instance, you can point out the various types of help to arrive and offer positive coping ideas.

Look at a memorial: Memorials tend to be beneficial to commemorate people and things that were lost. College memorials should be held short and appropriate to the needs and a long time of the overall college community. Children under four might not have the interest span to become listed. A known caregiver, friend, or comparative ought to be the child's friend during funeral or memorial activities.

Reassure children that college officials are making sure they may be safe: Children's anxieties abate when they know that respected adults are doing what they can to care for them.

Stay static in touch with parents: Inform them about the school's programs and activities to allow them to be ready for conversations that may continue at home. Encourage parents to limit their children's contact with news reports.

Look after yourself: You might be so active in assisting your students that you overlook yourself. Find ways for you as well as your colleagues to aid one another.

Signs of injury in Children & Adolescents

- Constantly replaying the function in their minds.

- Nightmares.

- Values that the world is normally unsafe.

- Irritability, anger, and moodiness.

- Poor concentration.

- Appetite or rest issues.

- Behavior problems.

- Nervousness about people getting too close.

- Jumpiness from loud noises

- Regression to earlier behavior in small children, such as clinging, bed-wetting or thumb-sucking

- Difficulty sleeping.

- Detachment or drawback from others.

- Use of alcoholic beverages or drugs in teens.

- Functional impairment: Failure to visit school, learn, play with friends, etc.

Chapter 6

How to Treat Traumatized Children

Dealing with children for traumatic encounters can prevent later problems.

What type of impact does contact with traumatic events have on children?

As the injury that children in various elements of the world might experience ranges from youth physical and intimate abuse, surviving all natural or political devastation, or being truly a see to an array of violent occasions, the emotional impact that stress can have on children may differ widely. Since injury responding is often subjective, there may be a multitude of ways that a kid can respond to being traumatized. What affects what sort of child might react to the stress includes:

the space of tie that the traumatic event has experience (an individual event that has ended quickly is less inclined to have enduring effects than long-term traumatic exposure) intensity of the traumatic event (experiencing or witnessing extreme physical or sexual assault) option of support resources opens to the kid afterward, whether through informal or formal public support services

Although some children have the ability to experience traumatic events without apparent ill-effects, the long-term consequences for most children can be serious, whether by developing later psychological problems or even physical problems, including drug abuse, personality problems, depression, or suicide.

Often, traumatized children can form full-blown posttraumatic stress disorder, and the latest version of the Diagnostic and Statistical Manual of Mental Disorders is likely to add a new diagnosis called Developmental Trauma Disorder (DTD) to be utilized for children who face repeated traumas while their brains remain developing. The suggested requirements for DTD include:

Publicity: Multiple or chronic contacts with a number of types of adverse developmental traumas.

Triggered dysregulation in response to specific, situational activates, can involve affective, somatic, or behavioral patterns of responding

Persistently altered attributions and expectancies. Lack of rely upon protectors, negative self-attitude, perception that future victimization is inevitable.

Practical impairments, Educational, familial, legal, or vocational impairments.

The necessity for a particular analysis for childhood trauma is due to years of research showing how common contact with trauma happens to be in teenagers. According to a 2002 study, including interviews with 1,420 children, one from every four adolescent children got experienced at least one extreme stressor, such being the sufferer of misuse or other extreme stress, sooner or later in their lives. Eighteen percent of the kids studied reported several stressors, and the analysts found that contact with one extreme stressor increased the chance of being contacted with additional stressors as time passes. These results have been backed by other studies displaying that children experiencing injury need treatment as quickly as possible to avoid or reduce long-term harm.

But which kind of treatment is most effective for child years' trauma? A recently available article released in Canadian Mindset provides an extensive overview of the various kinds of treatment designed for children who have acquired traumatic experiences. Compiled by a team of psychologists at the University of English Columbia and Kelowna, B.C.'s Youngsters Forensic Psychiatric Services, this article highlights that research into how effective different treatment options for coping with adolescent stress continues to be fairly limited in comparison to similar research in treating traumatized adults.

Cognitive-behavioral therapies (CBT) remain the best choice by most therapists, particularly because the available research is commonly far more powerful than research taking a look at psychoanalytic or purely medication-based treatment. While CBT was initially developed for injury in adults and later modified to children, the special needs that adolescent stress patients have influenced the introduction of treatment methods concentrating on children and children only. These treatment methods include:

- Multi-Modality Trauma Treatment (MMTT) -First developed in 1998. MMTT is dependent on the theory that stress at an age group can disrupt normal physical and emotional development, and uses age appropriate CBT ways, to help children cope with injury. Usually conducted in college configurations, MMTT programs have a 14-program format that ranges from psychoeducation, narrative writing (authoring the distressing experience), publicity and rest techniques, and cognitive restructuring. Empirical studies of MMTT show a marked decrease in stress symptoms with similar results for symptoms of major depression, anger, and anxiousness.

  The chief benefit of MMTT is that it was specifically developed for traumatized children, although the type of this program focuses on children who have experienced only one traumatic event. The worthiness of MMTT for dealing with polytrauma instances is much less well-researched.

- Trauma-Focused Cognitive Behavioral Therapy (TF-CBT) - First developed in 2006 by Judith Cohen and her colleagues. TF-CBT was specifically developed for children between the ages of three and eighteen.

Treatment programs using TF-CBT usually range between eight to twenty classes relating to the child by itself or the kid and a mother or father/caregiver. The primary goal of TF-CBT is to help children learn coping skills that will assist them offer with traumatic recollections. A component-based mode; TF-CBT, is structured using the acronym "PRACTICE." In treatment, children who receive psychoeducation, are trained rest skills, as well as effective appearance and modulation, and cognitive coping skills. Children are also motivated to use injury narration and also to cognitively process the stress, use in vivo contact with master injury reminders, have conjoint mother or father-child periods, and enhance basic safety. First developed for use with victims of intimate mistreatment, TF-CBT has been found to work with other types of stress as well and has been trusted in treatment configurations round the world.

- Stanford Cue-Centered Therapy (SCCT) - Produced by research workers at the Stanford College of Medicine's Early Life Stress Research Program. SCCT is a short-term remedy approach focusing on person therapy for children and dealing with injury. Made to treat issues with a child's cognitive, affective, behavioral, and physical working, SCCT uses cognitive-behavioral techniques, rest training, narrative use, and parental training. The purpose of SCCT is to lessen the child's mental poison and cognitions as well as level of sensitivity to distressing storage. Typically, fifteen to eighteen classes long, SCCT stimulates children to create coping skills, including rest and self-empowerment. By assisting children understand how trauma impacts them, they could control the way they respond to distressing reminders.

Despite its guarantee, SCCT requires considerable one-to-one therapy periods, which may be extremely time consuming. Case studies commonly limit research screening SCCT's value.

- Seeking Security - First developed for use with drug abuse as well as trauma in adults and adolescents. Seeking Protection has five basics: personal safety as important, integrated of trauma and drug abuse, concentrating on the client's needs, focus on the treatment process, and concentrating on cognitions, behaviours, interpersonal interactions, and case management. Seeking Security was specifically modified for treating children, and like the other treatment models uses psychoeducation, trained in specific coping skills, and cognitive restructuring. Parental participation is needed in a single Seeking Basic safety program, and training programs can be found online.

- Trauma Affect Rules: HELPFUL INFORMATION for Education and Therapy (Focus on)- First developed and tested on young offenders. Focus can be utilized individually or in group classes. The purpose of TARGET is to instruct clients to comprehend how trauma changes the brain's normal stress response and exactly how to control psychology giving an answer to trauma. THE PROSPECTIVE model uses the Independence acronym (concentrate, recognize triggers, feeling self-check, assess thoughts, define goals, options, and contribute). Most much like TF-CBT, one of the benefits of Focus on is that parents aren't mixed up in treatment. At the moment, most empirical research on TARGET's value has been young offenders.

Chapter 7

4 Methods to Start Recovery from Child Years Trauma

Bill's mom died suddenly of the aneurysm when he was six years old. Teresa was striked by an automobile when she was ten and spent a few months in a healthcare facility, often with no family support, frightened. Oliver's parents divorced when he was twelve, and he never noticed his dad again. Trauma; the unexpected event that explodes your daily life; a loss of life. a tragic incident. In the aftermath, there may be the grief itself- the dread, the physical pain, but also the battle to see the sense of what occurred.

Adults, of course, face the same problem, but children achieve this with a handicap. They don't have the complete functional, logical brain that the adult has. Their coping skills are limited, and their view of the world is understandably myopic and self-centered. I've spoken with an eight-years-old who, when asked why their parents divorced, immediately said that it was because they didn't end their research one night. Expenses, Teresa and Oliver will probably feel the same manner.

Just what a child does is make an unconscious or semi-conscious decision in what she or he must do to avoid this, whatever the "this" is, whether it is abandonment, pain, dread, or lack of control from happening again.

Here are the most typical options:

- I care for me:

The world is unsafe. I can't trust anybody, there's me, and there's me, and I look after me. I'm impartial; some say self-sufficient. I don't slim into human relationships, I don't start and let others in. Instead, I manage others when you are good and accommodating.

- "I'm compliant and passive."

The world is unsafe. Personally, I think I have little control, rather than much self-confidence. Therefore, I decided I need to go with others. They know much better than me, and sometimes when I'm overwhelmed, they help me out or inform me how to proceed.

- 'I need to remain alert."

The world is unsafe; therefore, I have to be hypervigilant. I am always stressed, always looking for risk, always anticipating the worst. A pal is late? He was previously involved in a vehicle accident. My partner hasn't called today? He's thinking of splitting up. People can misinterpret my stress and anxiety as irritability, to be always on edge, because I am.

- "I have to maintain control, and I'm angry."

The world is unsafe; therefore, nothing is going to sneak through to me. I'm in control, and nothing at all happens unless I say so. People give me trouble? I fight. EASILY don't agree, you're heading to learn about it.

These stances, carved away of trauma, take keep. They work, for the reason that they permit the child to go ahead in life and survive years as a child. The problem is that they linger and grow. A person may marry but never form true intimacy in their romantic relationship. Their passivity not only drives others crazy but maintains them from finding their life. Their nervousness keeps them residing in the near future, their negativity overshadowing the positive, their over-reactions disrupting their interactions or their anger dominates, and they have no control but are in a battle with the world.

The target is to become more flexible and less afraid. Change will come in a number of steps:

1. Start by realizing and going for a hard take-a-look at your position and its restrictions.

How will you view the world and exactly how to handle others? Using this method, you aren't only being honest with yourself; nevertheless, you begin to split up days gone by from present.

2. Get closure.

You intend to start to heal a few of the injuries by wanting to create closure, expressing what you cannot express at that time. Try writing a letter-in Bill's case, to his mom, for Teresa, to the automobile drivers or the doctors at a healthcare facility or simply her family who wasn't always there; for Oliver, to his parents-saying what you cannot say then. Then write another notice, from them for you, stating what it is you most want these to say that they may be sorry, it wasn't your mistake, that they cherished you. Make the characters as detailed as it can be, and allow you to ultimately jot down whatever involves the mind.

3. Step outside your comfort areas and patterns.

Time for you to be the grown up as opposed to the frightened child. Test out stepping outdoors your safe place: Speak up rather than being unaggressive, start and low fat in rather than being shut and isolated, concentrate on today rather than continually looking forward to the terrifying future, or test out allowing go of anger and control.

4. Get active support and help.

All this is simpler said than done, of course, and help and support are exactly what you hardly ever really received. sHere you might take the chance of seeking specialized help to aid and make those baby steps towards behavioral change; you might, on the therapist's advice, consider medication to help break through the cycle. It isn't about carrying it outright but carrying it out differently.

C h a p t e r 8

Looking after Traumatized Children

1. Know the Variation between Emotions and Behaviors:

People, especially children, can't be likely to control their emotions. It is 'okay' to feel mad, annoyed, or hurt. It is even 'alright' to feel the desire to do something on those emotions of madness or sadness. Children need to find out; however, they can control their behavior.

They want help separating emotions and activities. Teaching them positive self-talk can help them with this. In positive self-talk, you validate their emotions and also cause them to act appropriately.

Examples:

"I understand you are feeling angry; I would be mad too if someone said something mean if you ask me. You don't have to be mean back again, though. Suggest to them just what a strong person you are."

"Most of us feel bad sometimes, but it continues to be

important to take care of other folks with respect."

2. Be as consistent as you possibly can try the 1-2-3 approach to discipline:

1: Ask perfectly for what you would like the kid to do.

2. Repeat demand and inform them what the result will be if indeed they don't get it done.

3. Supply the consequence. It is good to provide a result that is linked with the behavior, what therapists call a "natural' outcome. For instance, no Television time until they end their research or clean their room.

However, additionally, it is important never to place a kid in a consequence hole they cannot escape, such as removing TV for times on end. Specifically, for more youthful, pre-teen children, it is almost always best to begin every day with a clean slate.

3. Teach children a number of coping strategies:

Children often don't learn how to make bad emotions

disappear completely except by exploding. Help train them that we now have different ways to feel better that won't create additional problems (for example, by getting back in trouble to be naughty, by harming another person, for damaging something they value by tossing it in a fit of anger or psychological upset).

Types of good coping strategies:

- Speak to a supportive friend or teacher

- Take action you enjoy; draw an image, play a video game

- Take ten deep breaths and think about something which makes you happy

- Exercise

4. Train Empathy Skills

This is also known as "interpersonal and psychological learning" (SEL) or "psychological cleverness." Children often need help understanding what it might be like to maintain someone else's shoes. Using role-play or similar video games, you can encourage children to believe about how another person would be sensed. You can keep these as switch functions in role play. You can even read them tales about other children and have them to believe how the kids in the story plot feel.

It could be useful to focus on teaching them the difference between different types of feelings. These exercises can be carried out in a classroom or other group established, but shouldn't be about any particular child in the course.

Chapter 9

How to help a Traumatized Child in the Classroom

Contact with chronic stress has tragic results on a few of our students. How do educators help?

Based on the Children's Defense Account, one in three African-America kids and one in six Latino men given birth to in 2001 will finish up imprisoned sometime in his lifetime. These staggering figures are tragic beyond words. However, + in order to improve them, we must change how exactly we perceive the kids behind the figures.

Among us (Joyce) helps educators and administrators do just this. Joyce works together with the SAN FRANCISCO BAY AREA Unified College District's College student, Family, Community Support Division, and many underserved SAN FRANCISCO BAY AREA colleges through her award-winning UCSF Healthy Conditions and Response to Stress in Colleges (HEARTS) program. While teachers sometimes visit a misbehaving child as a poor child or a mean or oppositional child, Joyce helps to see that the child is a frightened kid. Quite simply, the child's behavior is the consequence of chronic contact with traumatic occasions beyond his/her control.

Furthermore, to impacting behavior, trauma can wreak havoc on the student's ability to learn. Researchers have discovered that children who have been subjected frequently to trauma have problems with other social, mental, cognitive, and natural issues, including difficulty regulating their feelings, attending to, and developing good relationships, all of which make it very hard for a kid to achieve school.

But trauma publicity will not seal one's destiny. As the UCSF HEARTS program shows, there are things that teachers and other nurturing adults can do to mitigate the consequences of trauma and help students flourish rather than fail.

The scourge of complex trauma

Just about everyone has experienced some type of traumatic event in their lives whenever a situation so overwhelmed the brain and body was not able to handle it. Based on our inner and exterior resources, the majority of us were probably in a position to recover. However, children who reside in under-resourced communities where home and neighborhood assault, racial discrimination, and poverty are more prevalent can develop post-trauma troubles after experiencing what's called complex stress.

Complex injury occurs through repeated and continuous contact with trauma-inducing situations, the majority of which happen in a care-giving situation. Whenever a child can't rely on the close caregiver for comfort and safety, whether because of the caregiver's psychological struggling or because the caregiver is the foundation of trauma, that young person's capability to metabolically process and get over harmful stress gets significantly hampered.

The metaphor Joyce uses in her schools to clarify the consequences of complex trauma is that of a vinyl record. Whenever a track is played over and over, a groove is worn into the record; if, when playing a different track, someone unintentionally knocks the record player, the needle will miss over the record and land in the deepest groove, playing that music yet again. Even though you reach the finish of the tune, sometimes the groove is so deep the needle skips back again to play it once again.

Just like a needle on an archive player, complex trauma wears a groove in the mind. So when something nonthreatening happens that reminds us of the traumatic incident, our anatomies replay the distressing reaction, mobilizing us to either run from or battle the danger while shutting down other systems that help us think and reason. Should this happen again and again, we are more easily brought on into that dread response setting, never giving our anatomies time to recuperate. After a while, once we adjust to this chronic triggering, our behavior can appear crazy or rude when removed from the framework of trauma.

For a kid in a classroom, something as easy as the teacher bringing up his/her voice to get everyone's attention or accidentally getting bumped by another classmate can steer that child into this groove. When induced, the child's out-of-proportion psychological and sometimes physical response often makes no sense whatsoever to the instructor, making it problematic for the instructor to respond properly.

Approaches for Teachers

Just what exactly can teachers do to help students in their classrooms who have experienced organic trauma? In her educators, Joyce supplies the pursuing four strategies.

1)   Recognize a child is certainly going into success setting and respond in a sort, compassionate way. When you see a child that might be having a hard time, begin by thinking about, "What's taking place here?" rather than "What's incorrect with this child?" This simple mental change can help you understand that the college student has been activated into a dread response, which

may take many forms. For instance, the pupil might:

- Get yourself a "deer-in-the-headlights" look.

- Change red and clench his/her fists.

- Breathe quicker.

- Start moving because his/her body gets prepared to run or react.

- Burst into tears or look as though they're going to cry.

It's well worth noting that not absolutely all kids will act away. However, for individuals who do, once you identify the result in, kindly and compassionately reveal back to the kid: "I see that you're having difficulty with this issue," or "You appear like you're getting kind of annoyed," and then provide a few options of things the kid can do, at least one which should be attractive to her or him. This can help the kid gain a feeling of control and company and help her or him to feel safe once again. As time passes, if students who are experiencing something that is terrifying or harmful views that you genuinely give treatment and understand, then she or he could be more likely to say, "I want help."

2)   Create quiet, predictable transitions: Transitions between activities can simply trigger students into survival setting. That feeling of "uh oh, what's heading to occur next" can be highly associated with a predicament at home in which a child's happy, caring daddy can, unexpectedly, become a monster after he's experienced a great deal to drink.

Some teachers will play music or band a meditation bell or blow a harmonica to sign it is time for you to transition. The main thing is to create a regular around transitions so that children know: a) the actual transition will appear to be, b) what they're said to be doing, and c) what's next.

3)   Praise publicly and criticize privately: For children who have experienced complex stress, getting back in

trouble will often mean either they or a mother or father will get a strike. As well as for others, "I made a blunder" often means "I'm completely unlovable." Hence, instructors have to be particularly private when reprimanding these students.

To use Rick Hanson's words in his demonstration at the GGSC Summer Time Institute of Teachers: "Nurture the hell away of the children." Catch those occasions when the college student is doing effectively and point it out to build his/her self-worth: "Wow, I really like how you sat at the desk for a complete five minutes" or, "Many thanks for assisting your classmate." If you want to re-direct the behavior, do this privately and in relaxed voice as possible.

4) Adapt your classroom's mindfulness practice: Mindfulness is the perfect tool for counteracting the impact of an injury. However, it may also be intimidating for children who have experienced stress, as the practice

may talk about scary and unpleasant feelings and body feelings.

If you are using mindfulness in your class, you may consider using the next adaptations that the UCSF HEARTS program and Mindful Schools created:

Inform students that, if indeed they wish, they can close their eyes at the start of the practice. Normally, they should take a look at a spot before them so that nobody feels stared at.

Rather than focusing on how your body feels, have students concentrate on a ball or other object they're holding in their hands, what it feels as though, and appears like in their palm.

Concentrate on the noises in the area or of vehicles passing beyond your classroom, something exterior to your body.

By breaking mindfulness practice into these elemental components, the kid is much more likely to have a successful experience truly, and thus become more willing to apply in the foreseeable future.

5)   Look after yourself. This actually should be number one! The metaphor of gaining your air face mask first before placing it on the kid is most evident in this example.

www.ingramcontent.com/pod-product-compliance
Lightning Source LLC
LaVergne TN
LVHW051747050326
832903LV00029B/2768